Hysteria

'This is an utterly hilarious and brilliant show and I do mean brilliant. It sparkles, it shines and it lights up the mind' *Sunday Times*

'A custard pie of comic brilliance' *Time Out*

'A dazzlingly clever intellectual farce' *Guardian*

Terry Johnson's plays include: *Amabel* (Bush, London 1979); *Days Here So Dark* (Paines Plough at the Tricycle, London 1981); *Insignificance* (Royal Court, London 1982 and filmed, by Nicholas Roeg, 1985); *Cries from the Mammal House* (Open Heart Enterprises with the Royal Court, London 1984); *Unsuitable for Adults* (Bush, London 1984); *Tuesday's Child*, written with Kate Lock (Theatre Royal, Stratford East 1985); *Imagine Drowning* (Hampstead Theatre, London 1991); *Hysteria* (Royal Court, London 1993; revived Duke of York's Theatre, London 1995) and *Dead Funny* (Hampstead Theatre, London 1994).

HYSTERIA
or Fragments of an Analysis of an Obsessional Neurosis

Terry Johnson

Methuen Drama

Royal Court Writers Series

This revised edition published by Methuen Drama in 1995 in association with
the Royal Court Theatre and the Duke of York's Theatre, London.

5 7 9 10 8 6

First published in the United Kingdom in the Royal Court Writers Series in 1993
by Methuen, in association with the Royal Court Theatre, Sloane Square, London
SW1N 8AS

Methuen Publishing Limited, 215 Vauxhall Bridge Road, London SW1V 1EJ

Methuen Publishing Limited Reg. No. 3543167

A CIP catalogue record for this book is available from the British Library

ISBN 0 413 70360 6

Front cover: Design by Paradigm & The Loft.
Photo of Freud courtesy of Mary Evans Picture Library.

Typeset by Wilmaset Ltd, Birkenhead, Wirral
Printed and bound in Great Britain by Cox & Wyman Ltd, Reading, Berkshire

Hysteria

Setting

1938

Sigmund Freud's study at 20, Maresfield Gardens, Hampstead, London. A large, high-ceilinged room plastered in pastel-blue. The room is furnished richly: dark oaks and mahogany.

US french windows lead to a narrow porch and beyond, a well-kept garden.

USR the door to a closet. SR a large desk. DSR a wood-burning stove.

Along the wall SL, an armless analysis couch covered with a rich Moroccan rug and half a dozen cushions. On the wall above, another beautiful rug. Just beyond the head of the couch, a comfortable tub chair.

DSL the door to the rest of the house.

There are bookshelves holding fine embossed volumes, and every available surface holds antiquities from ancient Greece, Rome, Egypt and the Orient. The vast majority of these are small human figures in pottery, wood and bronze.

The setting should be naturalistically rendered to contrast with the design challenge towards the end of Act Two.

Characters

Sigmund Freud	An energetic old man.
Jessica	A woman in her late twenties or early thirties.
Abraham Yahuda	A large man in his sixties. An even greater weight and status than Freud.
Salvador Dali	A small tall Spaniard with a strange moustache and a talent for painting.
Figments	Love, Death, Guilt, Fear, etc...

The style of the playing varies as Freud's last thoughts, recent memories and suppressed anxieties dictate the action.

Hysteria was first staged at the Royal Court Theatre, London, on 26 August 1993, with the following cast:

Sigmund Freud	Henry Goodman
Jessica	Phoebe Nicholls
Abraham Yahuda	David de Keyser
Salvador Dali	Tim Potter

Directed by Phyllida Lloyd
Designed by Mark Thompson
Lighting Design by Rick Fisher
Sound Design by Paul Arditti

Act One

Scene One

Night. Rain beyond the windows.

Freud *asleep in the tub chair. Wakes and looks at his watch. A long silence.*

Freud   If you are waiting for me to break the silence you will be deeply disappointed. The silence is yours alone, and is far more eloquent than you imagine.

He turns in his chair and looks towards the couch. Double-takes when he sees there is no one on it. Looks around the room. Opens the door, peers out, closes the door. Goes to his desk. Hesitantly presses the buzzer on an unfamiliar Bakelite intercom.

Freud   Anna?

Anna *(a voice pulled from sleep)*   Yes, father?

Freud   Where's she gone?

Anna   Where's who gone?

Freud   It's um ...

Looks at his watch.

Anna   What is it?

Freud   Ten to.

Anna   It's ten to five. It's the middle of the night.

Freud   There was a girl.

Anna   Have you slept yet?

Freud   I had a patient.

Anna   Maybe you dreamed her.

Freud   I don't dream patients, I dream surgeons and publishers. What's this thing?

In front of his face hangs an electric light pull: a four-foot cord with a brass knob on the end.

Anna   What thing?

Freud   This thing in my hand.

Anna   Um...

Freud   It's just dangling here. It's got a knob on the end.

Anna   Mmm hmm?

Freud   What am I supposed to do with it?

Anna   Shall I call the nurse?

Freud   Shall I give it a pull?

Anna   No, just... leave it alone, father.

He pulls it. The lights go out.

Freud   Scheisse!

Anna   Father?

Freud   The lights have gone out.

Anna   Oh... that!

Freud   Damn thing.

Anna   It's a light pull. Ernst put it up this afternoon.

Freud   I hate the dark.

Anna   You should be asleep.

Freud   I know what's in it.

Anna   You need more, not less, as time passes.

Freud   The body maybe. The mind more than ever craves...

He switches on the light.

Illumination.

Anna   Shall I come down?

Freud   No, I'm fine.

Anna   Goodnight then.

Freud   Goodnight.

He switches off the intercom. He picks up his pen to write. Nothing comes. He gets up and lies on the couch.

I have been preparing, somewhat unsuccessfully, for my death which Yahuda would have me believe is imminent. I am inclined to agree with his diagnosis, but this morbid preparation is . . . difficult. I have never liked waiting for trains; gazing down the track, ever too anxious to glance in the direction of one's destination. I unfold and refold my newspaper, and fail to find anything of interest, even though the headlines roar. Like all the trains I ever caught, this one is running late. And so I wait. I re-arrange the luggage at my feet, grow anxious and inexplicably . . . impatient. I prepare and prepare and yet remain unprepared, because when the train arrives there will be no time to button the jacket or check the ticket or even say a meaningful goodbye. So until my inevitably fraught departure all I can do is wait, and re-arrange the luggage.

His eyes have closed.

A pause, then a figure appears through the rain and stops outside the french windows. **Jessica** *is sopping wet and initially appears waiflike. She wears a thin macintosh. Her hair hangs dripping to her shoulders. She taps on the glass.* **Freud** *opens his eyes. She taps again. He rises, disorientated, and discovers the source of the noise. She smiles.*

Freud   Go away. Go away. This is a private house, not Madame Tussauds. Please . . . go away! Oh very well, stay where you are, catch your death for all I care. What do you want?

He goes to his intercom. She raps frantically. He doesn't press the buzzer. She speaks. We don't hear her through the glass.

Jessica   I have to speak to you.

Freud   What?

Jessica   I have to speak to you.

Freud   I can't hear you. Go away.

Very matter-of-fact, she takes out a cut-throat razor and holds it to her wrist.

Jessica   I have to speak to you.

Freud *looks away. Thinks. Then goes to the french windows and unlocks them. He steps back. She enters.*

Freud   Stop there! Stop.

She stops. Closes the razor. Offers it to him. He takes it and secures it in a drawer.

You're sopping wet.

Jessica   It's raining.

Freud   That rug is from Persia.

Jessica   You told me to stop.

Freud   Get off the rug. How did you get into the garden?

Jessica   I climbed. Where the elm rests on the wall.

Freud   I'll have a tree surgeon to it first thing in the morning.

Jessica   Grazed my knee; look.

Freud   What are you, some sort of insomniac student?

Jessica   No.

Freud   You want me to read something you wrote?

Jessica   No.

Freud   Are you inebriated, irresponsible, rich? Is this a dare?

Jessica   No.

Freud   Do you know who I am?

Jessica   Oh yes.

Freud   Then what do you want?

Jessica   I don't know. I haven't yet decided.

Freud   Who are you?

Jessica   Don't you recognise me?

Freud It feels as though I should.

Jessica Yes, you should.

Freud We've met?

Jessica No, never.

Freud Please. It's late. Who are you?

Jessica I am your anima, Professor Freud.

Freud My what?

Jessica It's a psychological term denoting the denied female element of the male psyche.

Freud I know what it is.

Jessica Denied but desired.

Freud Damn nonsense, that's what it is. Did he send you?

Jessica Who?

Freud The lunatic. Jung the crackpot, friend of the gods?

Jessica No.

Freud He did, didn't he? This is his feeble idea of a practical joke.

Jessica No one sent me.

Freud Due to my advancing years I am quite prepared to come up against the odd figment of my own imagination, but I have no time for flesh and blood impostors. And I certainly refuse to confront aspects of my personality I did not even propose! Anima is tosh. Archetypes are a theatrical diversion!

Jessica I've not read much Jung.

Freud Not much is too much. How long have you been in the garden?

Jessica All night. Watching the house. The lights going out. Then one last light, illuminating you.

Freud Perhaps you should sit. Judging from your behaviour so far you are either dangerously impulsive or pathologically unhappy.

Jessica That's true.

Freud Which?

Jessica Both, I think. I have inverted morbid tendencies, I know. And a great deal of free-floating anxiety desperate for someone to land on. I am mildly dysfunctional, yes.

Freud You have recently been in analysis?

Jessica No, I've recently been in the library.

Freud If you are looking for a doctor, I'm afraid I have to disappoint you. My health deteriorates daily. The few patients I have left will soon be abandoned. I cannot add to my unfinished business.

Jessica What if I were desperate?

Freud There would be no point; I could never conclude. I will give you the name of a good man.

Jessica No. It's you I must see.

Freud Then you must be disappointed. I shall call someone to show you out.

Jessica Don't do that.

Freud It's very late.

Jessica What's wrong with your mouth?

Freud With this half, nothing. The other half I left in Vienna.

Jessica How careless of you.

Freud It's in a jar of formaldehyde. The surgery was drastic, but advisable.

Jessica I think I'd rather die than have a piece of me removed.

Freud Cancer cells develop a passionate urge to replicate. They abandon any concern for the function of their familial organ and strike out to conquer foreign tissue. They undermine the natural state, absorb and conquer! They are the National Socialists of human meat; best left, I felt, in Austria. Now, you must go.

Jessica   It's still raining.

Freud   How could you possible get any wetter? If you want to get dry, get home.

Jessica   I have no home.

Freud   I must insist. This is improper.

Jessica   I'll show you improper.

She takes off her coat.

Freud   What are you doing?

She takes off her dress.

Freud   Please, I am perfectly aware you wish to gain my attention but this is highly inappropriate. I shall call my daughter.

Jessica   And how will you explain me?

Freud   There is nothing to explain.

Jessica   Naked and screaming?

Freud   She will understand.

Jessica   But will the inhabitants of West Hampstead?

Freud   Now stop this. Your behaviour is totally unacceptable!

Jessica   My behaviour, Professor Freud, is as you first diagnosed. It is desperate, as am I!

She goes into the garden, still undressing.

Freud   Come back inside!

Jessica (*off*)   One hour of your precious time!

Freud   I will not be blackmailed.

She screams.

Thunder. **Freud** *takes her coat and pursues her. Brings her back inside, wrapped.*

Freud   Sit.

He moves a chair nearer the stove and ushers her into it.

Jessica   Thank you. I'm sorry.

She cries.

Freud   I shall try to help. But you will please remember you are in my study, not some boulevard farce.

Jessica   This isn't your study. Your study was in Vienna.

Freud   Who are you?

Jessica   Is it the same?

Freud   Almost. In the Bergasse it wasn't as simple to walk out into the garden.

Jessica   Why?

Freud   I was on the second floor. And there were many more survivors.

Jessica   Who?

Freud   The figures. I was forced to abandon some of them.

Jessica   They're beautiful.

Freud   I crammed as many as I could into rail crates for transportation. Each of them is quite unique but when packed in side by side, they lose their individual identities. Wrapped in newsprint they become . . . faceless.

Jessica   Are you in pain?

Freud   Yes. Are you?

Jessica   Oh yes.

Freud   I cannot take you on. I have no . . . time.

Jessica   It won't take long. I know what's wrong with me.

Freud   Self-analysis is rarely successful.

Jessica   You did it.

Freud   I had the advantage of being me.

Jessica   I've read all your books.

Freud   Have you indeed?

Jessica   Yes.

Freud   Understand much?

Jessica   Most.

Freud   Hmph.

Jessica   I didn't much enjoy *Jokes and Their Relationship to the Unconscious*. If you were going to analyse jokes you might have chosen a couple that were funny. I suspect you've no sense of humour.

Freud   Nonsense. Only last week I was taken to the theatre and I laughed three or four times.

Jessica   What at?

Freud   I believe it was called *Rookery Nook*.

He shows her a theatre programme.

Freud   English farce has a seductive logic, and displays all the splendid – ha! – anal obsessions of the English.

Jessica   Frankly some of your concepts are funnier than your jokes.

Freud   For instance?

Jessica   Penis envy. How in a thousand years of civilised thought anyone could imagine a penis an object of envy is beyond me. Those I have seen erect and bobbing seem positively mortified at their own enthusiasm. The only one I ever saw flaccid looked like something that had fallen out of its shell. Euugh. Why would anyone envy a squidgy single-minded probiscus that thinks it's God's special gift to those without.

Freud   You say you've done no analysis?

Jessica   None.

Freud I think you should begin as soon as possible.

She lies on the couch.

Freud But not with me.

Jessica Don't pretend you're not curious, Professor. You're longing to know what brought me here. There's nothing you'd like better than to see me barefoot in the head.

Freud You are mistaken.

Jessica Please.

Freud If I were to listen to anything you had to say, I would do so only because you are obviously disturbed, and only on the understanding that what we were doing was an assessment pending a referral.

Jessica All right.

Freud Very well.

He sits at the head of the couch.

Jessica How do we start?

Pause.

I can't see you.

Pause. She twists around. He looks at her with a well-practised neutral expression.

That's the point is it? That's part of it?

She lies back. Pause.

And silence? Is that part of it too? It is, isn't it? How many minutes of silence must you have endured?

Sunrise begins; a burst of birdsong.

I don't know how to begin. I was born in Vienna twenty-nine years ago. I am an only child. My mother was beautiful, my father the owner of a small printworks. We lived in a tall, narrow house. It was a strange house, as if built by a child, an unsteady tower of rooms like wooden bricks. My father had a bad hip, so he had a room made up in what was the parlour.

This was his room, at the bottom of the house. Anyway, I grew. I grew up, as you can see.

He makes a note.

You made a note, I heard you scribble.

She twists around.

What did you write, what did I say?

She gets the same neutral expression.

I see. Should I talk about now or then? Past or present? Both, I know, I'm sure, but which end should I begin?

She rubs briefly at the top of her breast, as if removing a splash of wine. A hysterical manifestation.

I'm here because I was sent. I wouldn't have come of my own accord. I have been married two years and my husband is concerned for me. He worries about my appetite, which is small, I admit. But I merely eat no more than I desire. My husband also wishes I spent more time outdoors; I prefer to stay inside. It is merely a preference, not an illness. So that's why I'm here. It is desired that I eat like a horse and live like one too, in a field if possible. If you could turn me into a horse my husband would be overjoyed.

She rubs.

What has he told you?

She gags.

Sorry. I don't like the outdoors. I don't need three enormous meals a day.

Freud   How long have you felt this way?

Jessica   It developed. Nothing sudden, nothing . . .

She rubs. Shakes her stiff fingers.

One just becomes happier indoors. Less interested in the taste of food. Really, I wouldn't be here at all if it wasn't for my wretched husband.

Freud   What is wrong with your hand?

Jessica   Didn't he tell you? My hand has been examined by specialists; neither could explain the problem with my fingers.

Freud   What is the problem?

Jessica   We thought arthritis, but we're assured otherwise. These three fingers have grown stiff, you see. They bend at the joints but will not move apart. The hand still functions, but it looks so . . . reptilian. It is intensely frustrating.

Freud   And there is no physiological impairment?

Jessica   None, I'm assured.

She gags, then rubs.

Sorry. Can you help me?

Freud   No. I cannot.

Jessica   I'm sorry?

Freud   And it is now time for me to go to my bed.

Jessica   That was hardly a full consultation Professor; we're barely beyond the symptoms.

Freud   I am as aware of the symptoms as you. And I am aware of the aetiology of your hysterical paralysis, as well as the traumatic triggers of your anorexia and agoraphobia.

Jessica   So soon?

Freud   I know these things not because your compulsive behaviour is unconvincing or because I am capable of completing an analysis in less than ten minutes, but because I published the facts of this case thirty years ago, and you no doubt, judging by your excellent knowledge of them, read it only recently. Now I am very tired, both of your games and of this evening . . .

Jessica   Please, don't call anyone.

Freud   Either you leave, this instant, or I'll wake the house.

Jessica   It was a stupid thing to do. I'm sorry. It's a case history that interests me, that's all.

Freud   So you are a student.

Jessica   Yes. Yes, I am.

Freud   Then your methods of study are most unorthodox.

Jessica   May we discuss the case of Rebecca S.?

Freud   Certainly not. You disturb me, you attempt to deceive me . . .

Jessica   Did I?

Freud   What?

Jessica   Deceive you? With the gagging and the . . .

She rubs.

Freud   Not for very long. Now if you've had your fun . . .

Jessica   Please, Rebecca means a great deal to me.

Freud   You have forfeited any right to my time and attention. Now you may go into the garden and scream or dance with the spring fairies, I care not.

Jessica   What would Dr Jung say if he heard you mention fairies?

Freud   He'd probably take me down the path and attempt to introduce us. Now go home.

Jessica   Please . . .

Freud   Not one more word.

Jessica   I'll go then.

Freud   Good.

Jessica   Could I ask one thing of you?

Freud   One thing.

Jessica   Could you lend me a pair of wellingtons? My feet are freezing.

Freud   Wellingtons?

Jessica   It's a lot to ask, I know. It's all right; I'll be fine.

Freud   Wait there.

Jessica   A pair of socks would be heaven; those thick sort of woolly ones.

Freud *leaves. Her manner changes. She opens the filing cabinet and finds a maroon file of flimsy correspondence. The sound of a door off alerts her. She opens the french windows wide, then hides in the closet.*

Freud *returns, with boots and walking socks, to find her gone. Looks out of the french windows, closes them and leaves his study, switching off the light.*

Jessica *comes out of the closet. Turns on the anglepoise. Takes a journal out of her coat pocket, and carefully puts it on the desk next to the file. Then she settles down to work her way through the correspondence; a concentrated, obsessive search . . .*

Lights fade.

Scene Two

Late afternoon. **Jessica** *has gone, as have the wellingtons. The room is reasonably tidy. Door opens and in marches* **Yahuda**, *an elderly Jewish doctor. He clutches a visiting bag and a bound document.* **Freud** *follows.*

Yahuda   No, no, no. I'm not here to debate with you. No one in your family, no friend, colleague or critic has ever convinced you you were wrong about anything. I'm quite happy to be argued into my grave, but I'm not about to be argued into yours. I did you the courtesy of reading this . . . babble, now you will do me the courtesy of listening.

Yahuda *stops at a chessboard in play and takes a move he's already prepared.*

Freud   I had wondered at your silence during lunch.

Yahuda   Being polite has given me indigestion. We are both old men.

Freud   Time is short.

Yahuda   I shall allow your ill health to temper my anger, but not to lessen my resolve. I shall not leave this room until you have agreed not to publish this work.

Freud   My friend . . .

Yahuda   That remains to be seen.

Freud   I see.

Yahuda   The first paragraph made my blood run cold. 'If Moses was an Egyptian . . .'

Freud   If.

Yahuda   You do not mean the 'if', Freud. None of your ifs are questions; all your ifs are excuses for the outrageous statements they precede. Your proposal is that the man who gave us the word of God, the founder of the Jewish nation was an Egyptian aristocrat.

Freud   A simple reading of the facts . . .

Yahuda   You deny his origins . . .

Freud   Any intelligent analysis . . .

Yahuda   You undermine the core of the myth!

Freud   Myth, precisely.

Yahuda   The symbolic expression . . .

Freud   The reflection of an inner desire . . .

Yahuda   Of a basic truth . . .

Freud   A perversion of truth, an attempt to satisfy . . .

Yahuda   Moses was a Jew! Moses was chosen! If Moses was not a Jew, then we were not chosen! Deny Moses and you deny us! At this time, of all times. At this most terrible hour . . .

Freud   I take away our best man.

Yahuda   This is dreadful stuff. It is irreligious, badly-argued piffle.

Freud   But apart from that, what did you think?

Yahuda   There can be no discussion. You may not publish.

Freud *takes a move on the chessboard.*

Freud   Yahuda, you are a believer I know, but also a scholar. And you do not believe that the Red Sea parted . . .

Yahuda   The this and that of the event . . .

Freud   Or that a babe floated down a river in a basket . . .

Yahuda   Are lost in the mist, the history. The mystery . . .

Freud   A babe in a basket would have drowned as sure as our nation on the ocean floor.

Yahuda   The myth, Freud. Remove the essence of the myth and you undermine the foundations of our faith.

Freud   Have you been talking to the lunatic?

Freud *discovers his desk disturbed, which begins to preoccupy him.*

Yahuda   'Religion is the neurosis of humanity'! You presume to find no evidence of God but in the imaginings of desperate minds. A few sparks in the head.

Freud   God is no more light in this darkness than a candle in a hurricane; eventually he will be snuffed out. But if one man's denial can explode him then that tiny conflagration would be a light far brighter than the guttering hopes he kindles in us. The death of God would light us not to hell or heaven, but to ourselves. Imagine. That we begin to believe in ourselves.

Yahuda   Damn yourself if you must.

Freud   I have to publish.

Yahuda   But remember one thing.

Freud   What?

Yahuda   You are not the only Jew who will die this year.

The pain **Freud** *has been suppressing overwhelms him. He fights and defeats it.*

Yahuda   Sigmund? Are you in pain?

Freud   Most uncalled for.

Yahuda   I shall examine you. A man in your condition should be making peace with his God and his fellow man. Not denying one and outraging the other. Fetch a towel.

Freud *goes to the closet.*

Freud   I have always believed unpleasant or embarrassing truths should not be hidden, so why this late in my life . . .

He opens the closet. An arm comes out and gives him a towel.

Thank you.

He closes the door.

. . . should I have anything to hide?

Stops. Realises. Looks back.

Yahuda   Know this, Freud. Unless you reconsider, you lose my friendship.

Freud   Good God.

Yahuda   Harsh, I know, but there it is.

Freud   Get out.

Yahuda   No need to be offensive.

Freud   No, not you.

Yahuda   Then who?

Freud   What?

Yahuda   You said: 'get out!'.

Freud   Indeed. Get out . . . your things. Get your things out of your bag. And please, examine me.

Yahuda *takes an instrument from his bag, and peers into* **Freud**'s *mouth.*

Yahuda   Be certain of one thing; there is precious little I would not do to prevent you publishing. If you had any guilty little secrets I'd hang the hippocratic oath and seriously consider blackmail. But not you of course. Half a century of meddling in other people's passions, countless female patients lying prostrate in front of you, and never a whisper of impropriety. No scantily-clad secrets in your closet, more's the pity. Oh, for a scandalous lever to prize you off your pedestal.

Freud   Ow!

Yahuda   Sorry. That certain things are hidden from us . . .

Freud   Ot?

Yahuda   Does not deny their existence.

Freud   Ot hings?

Yahuda   The minds of men, the face of God. You devote yourself to one invisible thing yet refuse to contemplate the other.

Finishes the examination.

It's as you thought.

Freud   Inoperable?

Yahuda   It's very deep now. I'm sorry.

Freud   No, if I had a God to thank I would.

Freud *grimaces.*

Yahuda   That's me prodding around. A pressure bandage?

Freud   Thank you.

Yahuda *removes from his bag a bicycle pump, a puncture repair outfit and an inner tube.*

Freud   What do you intend doing with that?

Yahuda   Mend my bike.

Finds the bandage. Ties it tight around **Freud**'s *jaw, with a bow on the top of his head.*

I wish you would consider morphine.

Freud   No.

Yahuda   Just a little?

Freud   Absolutely not. I would rather think in pain than dream in oblivion.

Yahuda   Oblivion may be precisely where you're headed.

Freud   I cannot end with an act of disavowal.

Yahuda   Then end in silence.

Yahuda *moves to the closet.*

Freud   No!

Yahuda   What?

Freud   Don't go in there.

Yahuda   I need to wash my hands.

Freud   Please. Use the one across the hall. This we use now as a closet. So much correspondence, so many books . . .

Yahuda   Hmm.

Yahuda *heads for the door. Stops on his way to examine the chessboard. Almost takes a move, but stops himself.*

You think everyone but you is a complete fool.

Exits. **Freud** *rushes to the closet and flings open the door.*

Freud   You said you were going, I thought you were gone.

Jessica *appears wearing her raincoat and wellingtons.*

Jessica   Get rid of your visitor, Professor. We have work to do.

Freud   We have no such thing. I have other appointments.

Jessica   Cancel them.

Freud   I said I would arrange a referral.

She goes back into the closet.

Would you please come out of there! Very well, you give me no choice . . .

He steps towards the closet. The raincoat hits him full in the face.

Freud   My God.

Yahuda *enters through the other door.* **Freud** *closes the closet door.*

Yahuda   I left my bike in the garden. I'll fix the puncture then I'll be off.

Freud Good.

Yahuda And you've another visitor; some Spanish idiot with a ridiculous moustache. Dilly, Dally?

Freud Dali.

Yahuda Doolally by the look of him. If you want a physician's advice, you're not up to it. You should be resting, not entertaining foreigners. Whose is that?

Freud Mine.

Yahuda Is it raining?

Freud Usually.

Yahuda Looks all right to me.

Freud The forecast was ominous.

Yahuda Indoor storms imminent?

Freud Yes. No. A possibility of flash flooding.

Yahuda I'll bring my bike in here.

Freud No.

Yahuda I can't mend it in the rain.

Freud It's not raining.

Yahuda You said it was just about to.

Freud No, I said there was the possibility of some weather. They weren't precise as to which sort.

Yahuda Looks awfully small for you.

Freud It shrank.

Yahuda When the last flash flood came thundering through your study, I suppose?

Freud Why don't you bring your bike through and mend it in the hall?

Yahuda As you wish, though upstairs might be best.

Freud Upstairs?

Yahuda   To eliminate any danger of sudden drowning.

Yahuda *exits through the windows*. **Freud** *opens the closet to return the coat*.

Freud   Now quickly, please. Out of the closet.

Jessica   If you insist . . .

Freud   No. I mean, stay where you are, and put your clothes back on.

A wellington boot flies out, which he catches.

Please. You must modify this behaviour immediately. This is a childish and ineffectual form of protest since I haven't a clue what you're protesting about.

Jessica'*s arm appears from the closet. Between her fingers, a letter of* **Freud**'*s. He moves until it's in front of his face, and starts to read it.*

I don't understand.

She stuffs the letter right down into the boot. **Yahuda** *re-enters pushing his bike and walking on one heel.* **Freud** *closes the closet.*

Yahuda   Your garden's infested with snails; I've just trodden on one.

Freud   Please, the rug.

Yahuda   Could you take this for a second?

He hands the bike to **Freud***. It is covered in snails and has a hot water bottle tied to the handlebars.*

Where's your bootscraper?

Freud   We don't have a bootscraper.

Yahuda   This is England, for heaven's sake. I'll find a stick or something.

Yahuda *exits. Crunch.*

There goes another one.

Freud *puts the wellington on the floor and uses his free hand in an attempt to retrieve the carbon copy.*

Yahuda (*off*)   What the devil? Freud! What's this?

Freud *rises, his arm inside the boot.* **Yahuda** *re-enters with only one shoe on, hopping.*

Freud   What's what?

Yahuda   I don't know what you call the damn things. It was in the middle of your lawn. When I was a married man they were made of sterner stuff.

Standing on one leg, he holds up **Jessica***'s slip. It falls in front of him.*

Dali (*off*)   No no no! Is all right; I see myself.

A sharp knock on the door. Enter **Dali***. A surprised pause, then sheer delight.*

Dali   So. Is true. What Dali merely dreams, you live! Maestro!

Freud   I can assure you there's a perfectly rational explanation.

Dali   He does not wish to hear it.

Freud   Who?

Dali   Dali.

Freud   Of course. Tell your Mr Dali I shall see him in just a few minutes.

Dali   But he is here.

Freud   Ask him to wait.

Yahuda   And there's more of it, underwear and all sorts.

Freud   It must have blown off the line.

Dali   But wait he cannot; he is here!

Yahuda   There is no line.

Freud   I know he's here, I heard you the first time.

Yahuda   Whose is it?

Freud   Um . . .

Dali   Excuse, but . . . I am he!

Freud   Oh, I see.

Yahuda   I'll put it on the compost.

Freud   No! Give it to me.

Yahuda   It's not yours, is it?

Freud   Yes. No. It's ... my daughter's.

Yahuda   Anna's? At her age she should be dressing for warmth.

He drapes the slip over **Freud***'s arm and exits on his heel.*

Freud   You are he.

Dali   And he is honoured.

A crunch. **Yahuda** *slips.*

Yahuda   Oh shit. There goes another one.

Dali *sits, pulls out a pad.*

Dali   You will not object?

Freud   What?

Dali   A first impression.

Freud   Ah.

Dali *sketches.*

Freud   It's not my bike. And my physician has piles, thus the er ... As for the snails ... they just took a liking to the bike, I suppose.

Dali   You have a head like a snail.

Freud   Thank you very much.

Yahuda *re-enters with a clean shoe and more clothing.*

Yahuda   Has Anna lost a lot of weight in the last week?

Freud   Yahuda, this is um ...

Dali   Dali.

Yahuda   We met in the hall.

Dali   You suffer from piles.

Yahuda   How extraordinarily acute of you.

Dali   Dali suffers also.

Yahuda   I know; I've seen your pictures.

Dali   You do not like the work of Dali?

Yahuda   You want a frank answer?

Dali   Always.

Yahuda   I find your work explicitly obscene, deliberately obtuse, tasteless, puerile and very unpleasant to look at.

Dali   Please. Dali has no need of these compliments, but he thank you very much.

Yahuda   I think I'll leave you to it, Freud.

Dali   This is the man; the only man who can fully appreciate the genius of Dali's spontaneous method of irrational cognition and his critical interpretive association of delusional phenomena. Wait.

Exits.

Yahuda   You want some advice?

Freud   What?

Yahuda   Don't let him get on the couch.

Dali *enters with a finished canvas, 'Metamorphosis of Narcissus'.*

Dali   Is for you. Now you tell me. Look closely, and tell me . . . from what does Dali suffer?

Freud   Eyesight?

Dali   Is true. This man is genius.

Yahuda   I'll mend this tyre and see you when he's gone. Here.

Offers **Freud** *a bundle of underwear.*

Freud   Thank you.

Yahuda   I'm damned if I can imagine her in them. In fact I'm grateful I can't imagine her in them.

Exit **Yahuda** *with his bike.* **Dali** *resumes his sketch.*

Freud   I'd really rather you didn't.

Dali   A thought, an idea from your head, it belongs to you. But your image belongs to Dali. Please.

Freud   I must insist. Put your pencil away.

He puts his pad down.

Dali   I have come to salute you . . .

Freud   Please don't bother.

Dali   . . . on behalf of all true disciples of the critical-paranoiac school of paint.

Freud   Who are they?

Dali   Dali. He is the only true disciples.

Freud   I see.

Dali   You are held in great esteem. We, by which I mean Dali and I, are engaged in a great struggle, to drag up the monstrous from the safety of our dreams and commit to the canvas. It is you have inspired this.

Freud   I am most flattered.

Dali   You say to dream, and there to search . . . is what I do. You say paranoia it transform reality to conform with the unconscious obsession, yes? So Dali gazes; is turned to stone, but and an egg. Narcissus flowers from the egg. Desiring to be reborn he only gazes at himself and dreams of death. Life in this state is as unlikely as a flower from an egg. Expressed with masterly technique and ingenious illusion of course, and this is what Dali does, and only him. Would you like me to hang him?

Freud   Oh please, don't bother yourself.

Dali   Is no bother. Is an honour. I put it here.

Freud   That's a Picasso.

Dali Picasso is Spanish. (*Removes painting*.) So is Dali.

Freud You like Picasso?

Dali Picasso is genius. (*Tosses painting*.) So is Dali.

Freud I much admire 'Guernica'.

Dali Picasso is communist.

Freud Yes.

Dali Neither is Dali.

Freud You'll have to forgive me for being frank. I am in a certain amount of pain.

Dali Divine.

Freud Distracting. It's been a pleasure to meet you.

Dali No. Dali cannot go. Not so soon. Let me descibe to you the painting I have just completed. It is called ... 'Dream Caused By The Flight Of a Bee Around a Pomegranate One Second Before Waking Up'. It depicts the splitting of a pomegranate and the emergence of a large goldfish. From the mouth of the fish leaps a tiger. From the mouth of the tiger leaps ... another tiger. From the mouth of this tiger, a rifle with fixed bayonet about to pierce the white flesh of a naked girl, narrowly misses her armpit. Beyond all this a white elephant with impossible legs carries past a monument of ice.

Pause.

You have to see it for yourself, really.

Freud Again, forgive my lack of courtesy ...

Dali Please, have none.

Freud Very well. I have always thought the surrealist movement a conspiracy of complete fools. But as you had the audacity to elect me some sort of patron saint, I thought it only polite to meet you. I now find I lack the energy even to be polite.

Dali Excellent! Dali has no concern for your health, no desire to be liked, and no manners. Until the moment he dies, he does as he please. And he refuses to leave.

Freud   I don't think I've ever met a more complete example of a Spaniard.

Dali *finds a snail on* **Freud**'s *desk*.

Hello, little snail.

He unsticks it, prizes it from its shell with the point of his pencil, and eats it.

It's not good. What sort of snail is this?

Freud   English garden.

Swallows it.

Dali   Is tasteless. Typical English.

Dali *looks around the room. Very nosey.*

Freud   Why then are you in England?

Dali   In Spain until one week ago, Dali paint and is contemptuous of the Fascist machine rolling towards. Then he think; no, this is all getting too historical for Dali. Immediately the desire to leave is enormous, and acted upon immediately.

Freud   Have you any idea when the desire to leave here might become at all substantial?

Dali   When Dali, being here with you, no longer feels real!

Freud   Shouldn't take too long then?

Dali   Please. Don't waste your precious time trying to analyse Dali; he is completely sane. In fact, the only one.

Dali *continues to look around, arrives at the closet and opens the door.* **Freud** *looks up.*

Freud   N . . . er . . . .

Dali *looks inside the closet and closes the door. Opens his mouth, closes it. Goes back to the closet. Opens it, goes inside, closes door behind him.*

Dali (*off*)   Buenos dias, mi amor. Eres hermosa y yo soy un genio!

Jessica (*off*)   How dare you!

A muffled blow, a cry and a crash. **Dali** *emerges, holding his genitals. Unable to speak for some time.*

Dali   The girl in your closet.

Freud   Girl? What girl?

Dali   The naked girl.

Freud   In my closet? Surely just a figment of your unique imagination.

Dali   She kick me in the phallus.

Freud   A merely hallucinatory sensation.

Dali   I have pain in the testicle.

Freud   Hysterical.

Dali   No, is not funny.

Freud   Obviously you are at the peak of your imaginative powers.

Dali   You think?

Freud *leads him to the door.*

Freud   Your fantasies have grown so undeniable, they push through the fabric of reality. It is imperative you return home and paint at once.

Dali   A naked girl in the closet of Freud with the hooves of a stallion; is good.

Freud   Visionary.

Dali   I shall dedicate to you.

Freud   Thank you. Goodbye.

Dali   The pain is transformed; is divine.

Freud   So good to have met you.

Dali   The honour, it is Dali's. I owe you my life.

Freud   An unintentional gift, I assure you.

Dali   Goodbye!

He leaves.

Freud Oh vey, what a morning.

Jessica *pops her head out as* **Freud** *grabs the clothing.*

Jessica Who was that?

Freud You must get dressed!

He tries to hand her her clothes, but **Dali** *re-enters and she slams the door.*

Dali No, no, no, no, no! I cannot leave.

Freud *hides the clothing behind his back.*

Freud Please, be firm in your retholution. Resolution.

Dali Dali is firm in his trousers. His pain has transformed, his member tumescent. Dali is obsessed. The vision in the closet must be his.

Freud No.

Enter **Yahuda**. **Freud** *spins.*

Yahuda Anna's? I think not. Give them to me.

Freud The what?

Yahuda The flimsies.

Freud I don't have them.

But **Dali** *can see them, and pounces.*

Dali Ahah! The garments of the Goddess.

He takes the bundle and buries his face.

Yahuda Has he met your daughter?

Dali She is a feast; you smell.

Yahuda *takes the bundle.*

Yahuda I'll do no such thing. Freud, there's about enough silk here to barely cover Anna's left shin. I intend to confront her with these.

Freud Ah.

Yahuda *heads for the door.*

Yahuda   And you'd better hope for a positive identification.

Freud   No, Yahuda . . . !

Dali   She fill my senses!

He throws off his jacket, grabs his pad, and opens the closet.

Freud   No!!

Freud *rushes for the closet,* **Yahuda** *escapes.*

Closet door closes behind **Dali** *before* **Freud** *can get there. He rushes to the other door, but it closes behind* **Yahuda**.

Jessica (*off*)   Get out of here!

Dali (*off*)   Ahh . . . mi amor, mi amor!

Jessica   Don't you dare!

A crash, and **Dali** *cries out. He emerges, reeling, a toilet seat and lid on his head. He reaches the middle of the room and passes out, unconscious.*

Freud   What have you done?

Jessica (*off*)   I am a defenceless woman and refuse to be intimidated by amorous Spaniards!

Freud   His arousal was entirely your responsibility. Should this man sadly regain consciousness, I can give you no guarantee of his behaviour unless you get dressed.

Jessica   Then give me my clothes.

Freud   Ah.

Jessica   What?

Freud   I have temporarily mislaid them.

Jessica   Well then . . .

Freud   Wait!

He removes **Dali**'*s jacket and throws it to her.*

Jessica   A woman has the right to sit naked in a cupboard without being propositioned.

Freud   I would defend your right, but not your choice of cupboard. Here.

Jessica   Thank you.

Freud   All right?

Jessica   Well, I don't think I'll get into the royal enclosure.

Freud   Please, stay hidden.

Jessica   If you swear to give me a hearing.

Freud   All right, I swear.

Jessica   When?

Freud   When Yahuda's gone. I'll give two knocks.

Jessica   It's bloody cold in here; I want more clothes.

Freud   All right! All right! I'll get you some.

Freud *closes the door on her again and starts to remove* **Dali**'s *trousers. Enter* **Yahuda**.

Yahuda   She's never seen them in her life.

He sees **Freud** *and* **Dali**. *Pause.*

You and I have to have a serious chat.

Freud   I was just . . . removing his trousers.

Yahuda   So I see. He appears to be unconscious.

Freud   Exactly. He began hyperventilating and fainted. I'm loosening his clothing.

Yahuda   He breathes through his backside as well, does he?

Freud   He was complaining of abdominal pains.

Yahuda   Really?

Yahuda's *professionalism takes over. He examines* **Dali**.

Freud   Most definitely. Indigestion maybe, but perhaps something very serious. Hopefully a ruptured appendix.

Yahuda   Hopefully!?

Freud   Well, I mean, something worth your rushing him to hospital for, but of course hopefully not, touch wood.

Raps twice on the nearest bit of wood, which happens to be the closet door.

Jessica *comes out of the closet.* **Freud** *steers her back in and closes the door, stubbing her elbow.*

Jessica   Ow!

Freud   Ow. That was the sound he made, just before he collapsed.

Yahuda *rises.*

Yahuda   This man has suffered a blow to the head.

Freud   Yes. He was going into the garden and hit his head on the doorframe.

Yahuda   As he fainted?

Freud   Yes.

Yahuda   Which?

Freud   Both.

Yahuda   That's not possible.

Freud   Yes it is. He was standing on the filing cabinet, fainted, and hit his head on the way down.

Yahuda   What was he doing on the filing cabinet?

Freud   I don't know. I wasn't here. I was already in the garden.

Yahuda   Doing what?

Freud   Chasing a swan.

Yahuda   Where did that come from?

Freud   I haven't the faintest idea. But it could have been the swan that entered the room very aggressively and forced Dali to retreat to the filing cabinet where he fainted in terror.

Yahuda   This is a complete farce.

Freud   A what?

Yahuda   If I saw it in a theatre I wouldn't believe it.

Freud   A farce?

Freud *picks up the theatre programme and ponders.*

Yahuda   Freud, I do believe you've finally lost your marbles. Sixty years of clinical smut has taken it's toll. Cross-dressing, violent tendencies and attempted sodomy . . . I'll keep it quiet of course, but I don't think you'll be publishing much else.

Freud   That is slanderous! What proof have you?

Dali   Owww.

Yahuda   I'll get my bag. When he regains consciousness I shall find out exactly what's been going on here.

Yahuda *exits.* **Freud** *close to panic. Knocks on the closet. He gets* **Dali** *by the ankles and slides him towards the closet.* **Jessica** *comes out.*

Jessica   You hurt my elbow.

Freud   Two knocks is the signal. Not one knock, not three knocks; two knocks.

Jessica   I'm not having him in here.

Freud   He's been rendered harmless. Just a few minutes, please.

Jessica   Added to those you already owe me.

Closes door as **Yahuda** *enters. Pause.*

Yahuda   Where is he?

Freud   He left.

Yahuda   He what?

Freud   Through the garden, went over the wall. What a morning. You were right; I should be resting.

Yahuda   He was only half conscious.

Freud   Self-induced trance; he uses it to paint.

Yahuda   Rubbish.

Freud   Exactly. How's your bike?

Yahuda What about the underwear?

Freud What?

Yahuda This stuff.

Pulls it from his pocket.

Freud Ah.

Yahuda Well?

Freud What did I say last time?

Yahuda You said it was your daughter's.

Freud Utter nonsense. She's far too . . .

Yahuda I completely concur.

Freud But she's hoping to lose weight. These are a sort of incentive to diet.

Yahuda What sort of a fool do you take me for?

Freud Yahuda . . . The truth of the matter is . . . Um . . . The Spanish lunatic came early this morning; we had given him permission to paint in the garden. He brought with him a young lady, a professional model . . .

Yahuda It's common knowledge Dali only ever paints his wife.

Freud His wife. She was his wife. The model was. His wife the model. He set up his easel, she unfortunately disrobed. To save you any embarrassment they were hurried indoors and Dali made a pretence of arriving after you.

Yahuda She's Russian, isn't she?

Freud Wh . . . .er?

Yahuda Dali's wife.

Freud She's er . . . is she? Is. Russian, yes.

Yahuda Where is she now?

Freud Oh, she . . . she left. Much earlier.

Yahuda What was she wearing?

Freud   Um . . . I give up. What was she wearing?

Yahuda   Well not these, for a start.

Freud   Well no, but I lent her a jacket and . . . my wellingtons.

Yahuda *eyes the wellington.*

Freud   She only took one.

Yahuda   I see. And then presumably she hopped half naked all the way down the Finchley Road?

Freud   No, she hopped across the lawn to the laburnum bush beneath which she had previously concealed her clothes. Then she left.

Pause.

Yahuda   All right, I believe you.

Freud   You do?

Yahuda   I'd believe anything of the godless avante guard.

Freud *collapses with relief.*

Yahuda   There's only one more thing you need to explain.

Freud   Yes?

Yahuda *wanders to the closet. Raps it once with his knuckles. His hand waves through the air as if to rap again,* **Freud** *stiffens, but the hand becomes an accusing finger.*

Yahuda   What's in the closet?

Freud   Absolutely nothing.

Yahuda   Don't give me that; you've been buzzing around it like a blowfly.

Freud *joins him at the closet.*

Freud   Papers, papers, a life's work . . .

Yahuda   Open it up.

Freud   I've mislaid the key.

Yahuda   Open this door.

He raps twice. **Freud** *instantly adds a third rap. Grins inanely.*
Yahuda *frowns, suspicious. Raps twice again.* **Freud** *adds a third rap.*
Yahuda *raps once.* **Freud** *raps twice.* **Yahuda** *dummies a rap.* **Freud**
raps twice, then hurriedly adds one.

Yahuda   What in God's name is wrong with you?

Freud *is desperately trying to remember the count.* **Yahuda** *raps again,
once, and strides away.* **Freud** *in complete confusion adds another one,
and also walks away. Then stops dead.*

Freud   *Scheisse.*

The closet opens. **Jessica**, *dressed in* **Dali**'s *clothes, walks out. Sees*
Yahuda's *back. As he turns, so does she, and attempts to return to the
closet.*

Yahuda   Ahah! Stop where you are!

She stops.

Over the wall is he, Freud?

Yahuda *closes the closet to cut off her escape. She keeps her back to him.*

All right, you bohemian buffoon; what have you got to say for
yourself?

She shrugs.

Don't give me any of your continental gestures. Just please
inform me what sort of a relationship you have with this man.

Another shrug.

Turn around, dammit, and face me like a man.

Jessica *fiddles with her hair.*

I swear he's got shorter.

She turns round. She's attempted to fashion herself a moustache. A pause.

Yahuda   All right, Freud; over to you. Let's hear it.

Freud   Um ...

Jessica   Dr Yahuda, the truth is ...

Freud   You wish to speak to me!

Jessica   That's true.

Freud   So in order for our conversation to happen, you did not leave with your husband.

Jessica   Who?

Freud   Dali; your husband. Because you wished to speak to me.

Jessica   That's right. I didn't go with my husband Dali, Dali my husband because . . . (*Dreadful Spanish accent.*) . . . I thtayed behind to thpeak to Profethor Freud which ith why I wath thitting in the clothet.

Freud   Besides; you'd had a row.

Jessica   Ith correct.

Freud   And you hit him on the head.

Jessica   Thith ith true.

Yahuda   With a swan, presumably?

Jessica   *Que?*

Yahuda   May I ask you a personal question?

Jessica   Thertainly.

Yahuda   What country do you come from?

Jessica   Thpain, of courth.

Freud *behind* **Yahuda** *now, gestures frantically.*

Jessica   Not thpain? No, I hate thpain. Spain. Spain? Plagh!

Yahuda   So?

Jessica   Sssso . . . I come from . . .

Freud *tries to look like Lenin.*

A very important city um . . . near Mount Rushmore. No, no. Only joking.

Freud *holds up an umberella and with his curved arm, tries to make a hammer and sickle.*

It rains a lot. Where I come from. England, it's ... no.

He stands in a Russian sort of way.

The people where I come from are very rugged because it rains so much.

He slow marches.

In fact many of them are dead.

He tries the same thing again, but more exaggerated.

Turkey? No. I'm just having you on. If you seriously want to know, um ...

Freud *stabs at his head with a finger, impersonating Trotsky's death.*

Where I come from ... They're all mad. The entire country is completely barmy. France! It's France! I'm French! No I'm not, what a stupid thing to say.

She's losing her patience with **Freud**. *He's losing his with her. He stands with his finger on his head.*

Mars. I come from Mars.

He does a Russian dance.

Or Russia, I don't give a t ... Russia! Russia? I come from Russia. That's where I come from. Russia.

Freud *dances a Russian dance and tears up the theatre programme.*

Very warm for October isn't it? Precious little snow.

Yahuda   You don't sound Russian.

Jessica   Oh ... *Vy mozhete skazat' mnye chuke proiti k zimnemu dvortcu? Dva kilograma svekly i butylku vodki. Da zdravstvuyet velikii Sovetskii Soyuz!* (Can you tell me the way to the Winter Palace? I would like half a pound of beetroot and a bottle of vodka, please. Long live the glorious USSR!)

Freud   Oh, bravo. That was brilliant.

Yahuda   Freud, be warned! I may be willing to suspend my disbelief this far, but not one step further.

Dali *comes out of the closet in his underwear.*

Dali   Excuse me please. Dali does not remove his clothings.

Freud   I can explain this.

Dali   Pretty girls remove their clothings for Dali, not versa vica!

Dali *pursues* **Jessica**. *She grabs her underwear from* **Yahuda**.

Yahuda   Freud, will you tell me why on earth you are consorting with these lunatics?

Freud   Patients, Yahuda.

Yahuda   I've been patient long enough!

Freud   No, these are my patients. A couple of mild cases to occupy my mind while I still have one.

Dali *grabs the shoulders of his jacket and lifts it slightly, momentarily concealing* **Jessica**. *He pulls it off her in a downward sweep.*

Jessica   How dare you!

Dali   Divine. You will pose for Dali, si?

Jessica   Certainly not.

She has discovered her frock in the bin, and runs back into the closet clutching it to her. **Dali** *follows.*

Dali   But your armpit, it is divine. I must make unto it the graven image.

He closes the door behind him.

Yahuda   I have other appointments. Under the circumstances you'll have no objection if I take this with me.

Freud   But there are no copies.

Yahuda   Good. Your obsessive professional enquires have obviously led to mild sexual perversion and a serious lack of judgement. You'll thank me for this.

Freud   But Yahuda …

Yahuda   No buts. On a personal level Sigmund, I sympathise. But a man of your degraded moral standing has no business publishing anything. Good day.

Freud   But I can explain.

Yahuda *leaves.* **Jessica** *emerges, buttoning her dress, and followed by* **Dali**.

Jessica   Professor Freud, I wish to continue the analysis of Rebecca S.

Freud   You have seriously damaged my reputation.

Dali   Where is your armpit?

Jessica   Under my arm. You promised we could discuss this.

Freud   The details of the case are fully documented.

Jessica   Not only by you.

She produces a small book.

Her real name was Miriam Stein. This is the journal she kept of her work with you.

Freud   So?

Jessica   I've simplified what she remembered of the sessions, and selected the most apposite passages. I'd like us to read it.

Freud   I have neither the time nor the inclination.

Dali   Please.

Jessica   What?

He waves some money at her.

Dali   To consider my request a professional proposition.

Jessica   Go to hell.

Dali   Your armpit only; name your price.

Jessica   I'm not for sale.

Dali   My Venus.

He kisses her hand . . .

Jessica   Professor?

Freud   It would be a pointless exercise.

And lifts her arm for a peek of her armpit.

Jessica   Get off!

Dali   On my knees.

Freud   I will have nothing to do with it.

Dali   Dali will do anything you ask.

Jessica   Can you read English?

Dali   Dali is perfect English. Not have got you ears?

Jessica   Very well. Read the passages underlined.

Dali   *Que?*

Jessica   We are going to reconstruct one of the Professor's case histories. You sit here. When we are finished you may have fifteen minutes to do what you will with my armpit.

Dali   Is a deal. I am to be the fraud of the great Freud, yes?

Dali *sits in the tub seat.*

Freud   No. I will not tolerate this.

Dali   Ah.

Jessica   What anxieties are prompting your objections, Professor? Read the passages marked with an F.

Dali   But if the Professor object to this worm presuming to embody him then this Dali cannot possibly . . .

Jessica *puts her hands behind her head.*

Dali   . . . refuse you my darling, and to hell with this man and his beard also.

Freud   Very well, if you insist. Get it over with.

Jessica   From the top of the page.

Dali   So. 'As you speak to me you will notice ideas will occur that you feel are not important, are nonsensical, not necessary to mention. But these disconnected things are the things you must mention. You must leave nothing unsaid, especially that which is unpleasant to say.' Maestro.

Jessica   Concentrate.

Dali   Of course.

Jessica   It's a warm day. I had difficulty getting here. The cab driver was reluctant to raise the canopy, and I cannot travel in an open cab.

She rubs her breast.

I don't like leaving the house. Walking across a field or a town square is a nightmare. I stick to the hedge or the edge of the wall, but even then there's this constant possibility . . . A wicker basket. Just came into my head. Is that the sort of thing?

Dali *is rubbing his nipple exotically.*

Jessica   What are you doing?

Dali   Is what it says here. I was gently rubbing my breast.

Jessica   Not your breast, my breast.

Dali   You rub the breast of the patient? Is not in the published works you did this.

He reaches out, she slaps his hand.

Jessica   She was rubbing her own breast.

Dali   *Que?*

Jessica   'I' is me.

Dali   Oh, *si. Si.* Apologise. 'Continue'.

Jessica   When I was young we had a wicker basket; I used to play ships in it. It was a picnic basket. I don't know why I've thought of this, but . . . my mother reading to us, the story of Chicken Little. A piece of the sky falls on his head. Bits of the sky falling.

Gags.

I hate the sky, the way the clouds scud. Something I've just remembered, God it was horrible, and I'd forgotten all about it. I'm lying in my Grandmother's garden. I'm almost an adult, I'm nineteen and she's told me if I lay still I'll get a spectacular surprise.

She rubs.

I remember this now. Suddenly the air is full of birds. Starlings. Not just a few dozen but thousands. A black cloud of starlings. A tattered sky and those horrible birds just . . .

She gags.

I run inside. And the starlings roost in trees all round the house and I sit curled up in a cold dark study in a leather chair and listen to the noise of the birds and my heart thudding. I'm scared of the starlings. I'm frightened of the birds.

Dali *applauds.*

Don't do that.

Dali   It says this. There was applause.

She takes the journal.

Jessica   There was a pause.

Dali   Oh, *si. Si.*

Jessica   I don't know why but I'm thinking now of a flame, a small, a candle flame . . . and it's burning upside down. I don't understand that. A heavy sky. Leaden. I'm afraid of the sky. No I'm not. It's not the sky, is it? It's that a bird might fly, might pass overhead. Not all those starlings, something far worse; one bird in a blue sky. That's what frightens me. The possibility of a bird.

She rubs.

Freud   Are you finished?

Jessica   No. Later they discuss her eating disorder and she free associates around food and meals.

She takes the book.

Rules her father had. Dessert spoon and fork lined up just so. The knife never ever put into the mouth . . . And eventually . . . I haven't learned this bit.

Freud   Please . . .

Dali   Shhh.

Jessica   'I am about seven years old. My father is giving a dinner party and I have begged to attend. I am on my absolutely best behaviour. The candles are lit and the mahogany shines. I ask my mother to pass the salt. I tip it, but nothing comes out. The salt is damp, so I shake the salt-cellar, and the silver top flies off. And the salt pours all over my food, and flicks down the table as I try to stop the flow. The guests all look at me. Some laugh. I feel the most unbearable humiliation. My mother brushes some of the salt into a napkin, but the food is ruined. My father's face is chiselled in stone, so I pick up my knife and fork and I eat. I pretend it's all right. I eat until my gums sting and my eyes water. I run upstairs, I throw up, and I put myself to bed. The bed is cold. I listen to the guests leaving and pray my father doesn't climb the stairs.' There was a silence, then you asked Rebecca how often she had intercourse with her husband.

Freud   I refuse to participate in this any further.

Jessica   We leap a few sessions and find . . .

Freud   No! You will leave now, please.

She opens a desk drawer and pulls out her razor.

Jessica   I have to finish this. Help me finish it.

Dali   Please. I say something?

Jessica   Yes?

Dali   Goodbye.

Jessica   Stay where you are.

Dali   Just here?

Jessica   Just there.

Dali   Is good. Is very nice just here. No need to move at all, never.

Freud   Give me the razor.

Jessica   Let me do what I have to do and then I swear, I'll disappear.

Dali   Is good to give it to him. Is better to keep it though. Wow, it's really nice just here, isn't it?

Jessica   Sit down. It's a few weeks later and her gagging has greatly reduced; she has successfully related it to the taste of salt, and thus to the trauma of the dinner party. From there.

Dali   'I wish you to concentrate on your fear of birds. What thoughts come to you?'

Jessica   The smell of leather. Mahogany. A candle flame. Of course, at the dinner party the candle flames were reflected in the polished wood. They were upside down.

Dali   'And the birds?'

Jessica   Oh, birds, eggs, boiled eggs . . . the picnic basket. I'm sick to death of that picnic bask . . .

Dali   A pause.

Jessica   I'm eating a boiled egg at a picnic. My whole family is there. My father has refused to undo his collar. It is very hot. He offers me salt in which to dip my egg. I of course decline. I'm in my late teens by now, I think of myself as very demure. I am dressed in white, and it's . . . it's my father's birthday! I feel good towards him. I feel he likes me now. He gives me an odd stiff smile. I'm sure if we were alone we could talk together now. I wish we were alone. A long way off a child is crying. A bird flies overhead. My father calls my name. Miriam. I look up and smile and *no*!

She cries out in disgust. Rubs violently. Gags.

Jessica   It's all over me; my dress, my breast.

Dali   'What is this?'

Jessica   A bird, a filthy bird. A streak of white, a flash of green, it's warm and wet and it's on my breast. An unspeakable mess; it's bird excrement.

Dali   'Relax.'

The fit continues.

'You are here, you are safe. He embraces her.'

The fit continues.

Is your line.

Freud   He embraces her!

Dali   Oh, *si*. Is allowed?

Freud   Yes, is allowed.

Dali *embraces her. She calms down.*

Jessica   It's all over my fingers and my beautiful new breast. Dress. All afternoon my fingers feel . . . sticky. Stuck together. All the way home, I hide my hand. And my father, all the way home, never once looks at me.

Pause.

Is that how it was? Her fit?

Dali   Was magnificent.

Jessica   Is that how it was?

Freud   Similar.

Jessica   And did you embrace her?

Freud   Yes.

Jessica   She says . . . (*Reads*.) 'I clung to him to prevent myself falling through the door that had opened up beneath me and through which I had seen that summer's day so clearly. And the door righted itself and I knew it was now my choice to step through and remember whatever I wished. I am so deeply and eternally grateful to this man.'

Freud   Transference is common to all successful analyses.

Jessica   They all fall in love?

Freud   Without exception.

Dali   Wow.

Freud   And the gift that must be returned is an acceptance of that love, with no love returned, no demands made, no respect diminished.

Jessica   You never loved in return?

Freud   Of course not.

Jessica   She felt euphoric at the revelations tumbling from her past. And the symptoms began to disappear. What continued to disturb her were your questions about her intimate affairs. She admitted a distaste for copulation and acknowledged her husband's frustration, but every week you insisted she spoke of these things.

Freud   This is indelicate.

Jessica   We've reached the crucial session.

Freud   Whatever confidences you are about to reveal from this poor woman's private reminiscences, I can assure you that no impropriety ever took place between us.

Jessica   I'm not accusing you.

Freud   You were about to do so.

Jessica   It's obviously something you feel very defensive about . . .

Freud   How dare you!

Jessica   But I have no intention of making any such accusations.

Freud   Then what is your point?

Jessica   One more visit. The seventh. Things are not good. The gagging has returned and she finds it impossible to keep any food down. Her fingers are useless, and her wiping tic incessant and exaggerated. She's distraught that in spite of all she's learned, she's iller than ever.

Freud   When she arrived. Not when she left.

Jessica   She was very angry with you, very angry, and you sensed this. Didn't you?

Freud   Of course.

Jessica   And you encouraged her to express her anger, didn't you?

Freud Of course.

Jessica And did she? Did she? *Did she*?!

She hits him.

Dali No.

Freud It's all right. Yes she did.

Jessica I'm almost there. Almost there now.

The hysterical symptoms take hold of her, more exaggerated and more frequent. Other physical tics manifest themselves. She returns to the couch in an increasingly distressed state.

Dali Is what page, which, I don't know.

Jessica *moans loudly, an agonised exhalation that frightens* **Dali**.

Dali Please.

Freud It's all right.

Dali To help me, please.

Freud She's all right. She'll be all right.

He takes the chair.

Rebecca? Rebecca? What is wrong with your hand?

Jessica The excrement.

Freud Your breast?

Jessica And my fingers; covered in shit. I know! I know! But I can't, it's . . . I'm still so angry!!

Freud Angry.

Jessica Yes, angry.

Freud At the bird?

She breaks down. Gags.

Freud What is wrong with your mouth?

Jessica The taste.

Freud Describe the taste.

Jessica   The taste of salt. It's salt. Everything tastes of salt!! I'm filthy with this shit and all I can taste is salt.

Freud   Associate. The taste of salt.

Jessica   A candle burns upside down; it's reflection in mahogany. The dinner party.

Freud   A candle?

Jessica   Put it out. No; the . . . cutlery.

Freud   Tell me about the candle.

Jessica   It's in the middle of the dining table.

Freud   No, the other candle.

Jessica   What other? There is no other candle. Except the one I was allowed. I hate the dark; my mother allows me a candle. My father thinks it a waste. He will open my door and bark 'put it out'. The door opens . . . Pause. She's still for a moment. Don't put the knife in your mouth. He opens the door. Put out the candle. The taste of salt and my . . . my fingers.

She sobs quietly.

Freud   Why are you crying?

Jessica   I don't know.

Freud   I think you know. The candle is burning.

Sobbing openly, growing in violence.

Jessica   The candle is burning. He opens the door. He says 'put it out'. Put it . . . ! Put it . . . !

Freud   That's enough.

Jessica   The candle is not upside down! It's me, I'm upside down! My head is hanging over the side of the bed. Put it . . . !

Freud   That's enough now. Rebecca.

Jessica   Put it in your mouth!!

Incapable of continuing, she stops.

Freud   Rebecca. No more now.

Jessica   She remembered. She remembered. The mess on her breast and her fingers and the taste of salt.

Dali   Don't cry. Please.

Jessica   I'm sorry. I'll be all right in a minute.

Dali   What was this?

Freud   She had remembered being raped. Orally. Before she was five years old.

Jessica   The taste of salt was the taste of her father's semen. The filth on her breast that she tried to clean off was his. When she woke in the morning her fingers were stuck together. She was carried from your study, and slept for three days.

Freud   Over the next few sessions she released a great deal of anger and began to examine her feelings of guilt. She regained her appetite and her physical symptoms disappeared.

Jessica   She was ecstatic. (*Reads*.) 'For the first time in my life I am happy. I feel there is nothing now in my past that can throw a shadow over my future. This morning I shall prepare ... a picnic basket.'

Freud   However. The events that Rebecca had remembered ...

Jessica   Miriam! Her name was Miriam.

Dali   And she and her husband?

Jessica   Oh, eventually. Sexual relations were resumed. Which I suppose means I also have you to thank, Professor Freud.

Freud   What for?

Jessica   My life.

Freud   She was your mother.

Jessica   You cured her.

Freud   You have her mouth.

Jessica   You released her, enabled her. You were her saviour.

Dali   Is good. You come not to criticise, but to pay homage.

Jessica   What did you think, Professor?

Freud *lowers his head, thinking.*

Jessica   When I found her journal I had to come.

Dali   I like this. Your mother is cured and is a happy ending, yes?

Jessica   Not really, no.

Dali   No?

Jessica   Nine years later my mother died in the washroom of an insane asylum near Paris. She took a rubber tube they used for giving enemas and swallowed it; force fed it to herself. The other end she attached to a faucet, turned the tap, and drowned. In case you're still wondering Professor, that is why I'm here.

Act Two

The same. Twilight.

Dali Is serious now, yes?

Jessica Yes.

Dali I go put my trousers on.

He retires to the closet.

Freud I had no knowledge of your mother's death.

Jessica That's hardly surprising. Rebecca S. has little in common with Miriam Stein. Your patient was a successful case history; my mother a suicidal hysteric.

Freud The last time I saw her she returned to inform me of her health and happiness.

Jessica She was pregnant, with me.

Freud She had had, she said, a wonderful year.

Jessica 1897.

Freud What?

Jessica 1897.

An air-raid siren sounds. They look up. **Dali** *comes out of the closet, crosses and exits out the door.*

Dali Scuse.

Freud *draws the curtains. The intercom buzzes.*

Freud Yes?

Anna Father? We are going to the shelter.

Freud I have been thrown out of my home, shunted over Europe, and shipped across the Channel. No further.

Anna It's just down the garden.

Freud   I shall soon be spending a substantial amount of time in a hole in the ground. I don't intend to climb into one while I can still argue the toss.

Anna   Very well. But if there are bombs, get under the desk.

Freud   Don't be absurd.

He switches it off. **Dali** *enters in a gasmask.*

Dali   Scuse.

And goes back into the closet.

Freud   If you would prefer to shelter . . .

Jessica   I'd prefer to talk. I don't have many vivid memories of my mother. She never went out, and she ate alone. I never took a walk or ate a single meal with her. I don't remember her treating me badly, but nor do I have the faintest recollection of her loving me. My father had her committed when I was five years old. I never saw her again. Are you aware of what you did to her?

Freud   I?

Jessica   On that final visit.

Freud   She was strong, healthy, and functioning well.

Jessica   Obviously you had managed to turn her into a horse.

Freud   Her symptoms had subsided, her neuroses were negligible.

Jessica   And my father could penetrate her whenever he so desired. Thank you doctor; my wife is cured.

Freud   Not cured no, rendered capable. Remarkably so, considering.

Jessica   What?

Freud   That her analysis was incomplete.

Jessica   Was it? Was it?

Jessica *takes a book from the shelf. Opens it at a page she's previously marked.*

The Aetiology of Hysteria. 1896. 'In every case the cause of hysteria is a passive sexual experience before puberty, i.e., a traumatic seduction.' This is what you wrote.

Freud   Yes it is.

Jessica   No equivocation, no trace of doubt. You wrote to your friend Fliess; 'Have I revealed the great clinical truth to you? Hysteria is the consequence of presexual shock.' That's what you believed.

Freud   Yes it is.

Jessica   And you published.

Freud   Yes I did.

Jessica   You were absolutely certain.

Freud   Yes I was.

She pulls a crumpled letter from a wellington boot.

Jessica   One year later. 'My Dear Fliess. Let me tell you straight away the great secret which has been slowly dawning on me in recent months. I no longer believe in my neurotica.'

Freud   What is the point you wish to make?

Jessica   One year later and you what? You changed your mind!

Freud   1897 may have been a wonderful year for your mother, but it was torture for me.

Jessica   Why?

Freud   None of my clinical cases would come to a satisfactory conclusion; the results of my analyses were imperfect therapeutically and scientifically.

Jessica   So when my mother returned to tell you of her happiness and my genesis . . . you took back your blessing!

Freud   Previously I had believed that sexual abuse was the root cause of all her unhappiness. A year later I knew this was not the case.

Jessica   You told her she never had been abused. That her memory of abuse was a fantasy.

Freud   That is so.

Jessica   You told her her father did not seduce her; that it was she who desired to seduce her father.

Freud   That is something of a simplification.

Jessica   But by the autumn of that year, all the childhood seductions unearthed by your patients; none of them had ever occured.

Freud   In the unconscious there is no actual reality. Truth cannot be distinguished from emotional fiction.

Jessica   So you abandoned them.

Freud   I abandoned the theory. It was false and erroneous.

Jessica   Was it? When you proposed that abuse was the root cause of so much mental illness you needed the support of the intelligentsia, and instead you were laughed at and reviled. Publishers closed their doors. Anti-Semitic tracts appeared. Everything you'd worked for was threatened. Your patients were the daughters and wives of wealthy and privileged men. Whom you began to accuse of molesting their own children. And then suddenly, you decide you were wrong. How convenient.

Freud   Convenient? To have shared a revelation and then discover it was false? All I had to steer myself through that terrible year was my integrity. I have never bowed to outrage or to ignorance.

Jessica   Had you not changed your mind, the outraged and ignorant would have crucified you!! My own grandfather, who my mother accused, was friend or acquaintance to every publisher in Austria!

Freud   You are accusing me of the most heinous opportunism!

Jessica   Yes. Yes I am!

Freud   Do you realise how many women retrieved 'memories' of abuse while lying there?

Jessica   Many.

Freud   More than many. You will forgive my astonishment at being asked to believe that sexual perversion was prevalent amidst the genteel classes in epidemic proportions. I was proposing a virtual plague of perversion. Not merely socially unacceptable; fundamentally unthinkable!

Jessica   My mother . . .

Freud (*harsh*)   Your mother was a hysteric! Her memories of seduction were wishful fantasies based on her unconscious desire to possess her father, his penis and his child.

Jessica   How can you believe that?

Freud (*rapid*)   At the crucial age of seven, if my memory serves me, her own mother dies. She believes herself to be guilty of killing her mother to attain her father. Her development is arrested, her guilt repressed along with her desires.

Jessica   I've read all this.

Freud   Years later she develops the hysterical symptoms and the fantasies begin to emerge alongside the memories.

Jessica   She was not just another case history! She was my mother and I know that she was . . .

Freud   You know nothing!! You are obsessive and ignorant! Your theories are simplistic. Your motives malicious. I have given you quite enough of my time. Thank you.

Jessica   Why so angry, Professor Freud?

Freud   I AM ANGRY WITH NO ONE!!

Dali (*off*)   Arrgh!

He bursts out of the cupboard, holding his forefinger before him like a beacon. It's bleeding.

Maphu mothur ufgud! Haffmee!

He tears off his gasmask.

Dali Is my blood.

Jessica What have you done?

Dali Please, call an ambulance and alert the hospital. Look, is my blood. Is coming out of my finger.

Jessica Calm down. Have you first aid?

Freud In the drawer.

Dali I sit in the closet, I notice on the wall the piece of . . . how you say this? Nasal mucus. Fastened to the wall with much exhibitionism. Very old; a previous owner I am sure. Is pearly green with a sharp point that makes a gesture which is a trumpet call for intervention. Is disgusting, so I take my courage, wrap my finger in handkerchief and savagely tear the mucus from the wall! But is hard and steely point like a needle! Look; is here. It penetrate between the nail and the flesh! All the way down. Is great painful.

Jessica I'm sure it is.

Dali Is to the bone.

Jessica I'll pull it out.

Dali Please. Be carefully.

She pulls out the mucus. Wraps it in handkerchief.

Dali Argh!

Jessica Here; disinfect it with this.

Dali Is throbbing.

Jessica Be a brave soldier.

Freud *begins reading his letters to Fliess.*

Dali Is go boom, boom, boom; the music of perfidious infection. Argh!

Jessica What?

Dali Is still there! The pointy part is still deep down. I see it through the nail. Get it out.

Jessica It's too deep.

Dali No! Is will be infected. Is death. Death weigh in my hand like ignominious kilo of gesticulating worms.

Jessica It's only a splinter.

Dali Is unknown nasal mucus! This finger is swelled. This hand is begin to rot. Please, get me to a hospital. I have it surgically dismissed at the wrist. Buried. It decompose without me.

Jessica It's not snot anyway.

Dali It's not?

Jessica No, it's not.

Dali *Si si!* It's snot. Is what I said.

Jessica It's a bit of glue.

Dali It's not.

Jessica No. A drop of wood glue.

Dali Oh. *Si.*

Jessica You'll survive.

Dali Is possible. Thank you.

Freud *replacing letters in cabinet.*

Jessica Don't put those away; I haven't finished reading them.

Freud The discovery of your mother's sad history has been very traumatic for you, but whatever quest you have set yourself is a hopeless one. I have nothing to hide. Indeed, to hide nothing has been my sole quest.

Jessica Then let me have the letters!

Freud (*off*) Certainly not!

Yahuda *enters, dressed for outdoors.*

Yahuda Freud. Apologies for this but I must beg hospitality. Every time I turn on my bicycle lamp I'm yelled at by cockney plebians in flat caps and armbands. It's pitch black; I can't get home.

Freud   Nor can Mr Dali and his wife.

Dali *looks for his wife.*

Dali   Please?

Jessica   I think it's time Dr Yahuda was told the truth.

Freud   No.

Jessica   Mr Dali and I are not married.

Freud   But share a common law agreement. It's a changing world, Yahuda.

Jessica   We met for the first time earlier this afternoon.

Freud   A rapidly changing world.

Yahuda   Your private lives are your own affair.

Jessica   It is true that I am Russian.

Freud   Is it? Good.

Jessica   And I have been engaged by Professor Doctor Freud to translate some of his letters.

Freud   Yes, that's it. Precisely.

Jessica   And those are the only ones I haven't done.

Freud   Ah.

Jessica   May I continue?

Freud   No.

Jessica   Why not?

Yahuda   Why not?

Freud   Very well. If you must.

Jessica *takes the letters.*

Jessica   Thank you, Professor.

She retires to read. **Dali** *sketches her.*

Freud *notices his manuscript under* **Yahuda***'s arm, and takes it.*

Freud   And this, I believe, is mine.

Yahuda   I should have dropped it down a drain. It's a bad time to discourage men from putting their faith in God.

Freud   On the contrary.

Yahuda   Have you read this evening's paper?

Freud   No.

Yahuda   Then do so.

Slaps it at him.

Seven thousand Jewish shops looted. Three hundred synagogues burned to the ground. Babies held up to watch Jews being beaten senseless with lead piping. They are calling it *Kristallnacht.*

Freud *takes the paper.*

Yahuda   Apparently Goering is displeased that so much replacement glass will have to be imported. He said they should have broken less glass and killed more Jews. Have you heard from your sisters?

Freud   No.

Jessica   Sisters?

Freud   Four elderly ladies. We have not been successful in our attempts to bring them out.

Yahuda   Don't blame yourself.

Freud   It is entirely my fault.

Yahuda   No.

Freud   If I myself had left sooner, I would have been more able to make suitable arrangements.

Yahuda   You've done what you can.

Freud   I do not believe I shall see them again.

Yahuda   They say it is to be the last war. Do you think so?

Freud   My last.

Yahuda   You lead us from the wilderness and then abandon us. Why for the love of God throw doubt upon him now?

Jessica   Why indeed?

Freud   Have you finished with those?

Jessica   It couldn't mean you wish to be doubted, could it?

Freud   I wish to be left in peace!

Jessica   You doubt nothing?

Freud   Nothing!

Yahuda   What are you reading?

Freud   Nothing.

Jessica   You should read them also.

Freud   Yahuda; a cigar?

Yahuda   You stink of cigars.

Freud   No more lectures, please. I have already smoked myself to death. I now do it purely for pleasure.

Freud *lights a cigar.*

Jessica   This one's interesting.

Yahuda   Is it?

Freud   No, it isn't. Yahuda, come with me. I need some fresh air.

Yahuda   What about the Luftwaffe?

Freud   You think from two thousand feet they could spot the butt of an old cigar?

Yahuda   With my luck they'll recognise you instantly.

Yahuda *and* **Freud** *exit into garden.*

Dali   What are you looking for?

Jessica   I don't know, but I think he does.

Dali   Please. Lift your arm. You owe this.

She lifts her arm. He draws while she continues reading.

Dali   Later, you and I; we have dinner of seafood. Crush the complacent shell of crab and lobster and eat the flesh while still surprised. Then, break into National Gallery and visit the London Exhibition of Degenerate Art courtesy of Adolph Hitler, then tomorrow at dawn, by the light of the sun rising over Primrose Hill I shall render your armpit through my eyes and into history.

Jessica   I'm washing my hair.

Dali   Heaven, to Dali, is the depilated armpit of a woman.

Jessica   Forget it. That's the hair I'm washing. Do you expect to make love to all your models?

Dali   Never. Sometimes they make love to one another, but Dali only this he observes.

Jessica   You don't like being touched, do you? I noticed earlier. It makes you anxious. It makes you squirm.

Dali   Please.

Jessica   Do you make love to your wife?

Dali   We did this, but no more.

Jessica   Why not?

Dali   The last time we made love, Dali, at the climax of his passion, cried out the name of another.

Jessica   Your mistress?

Dali   No, my own. Gala she say is over, and goes fuck fishermen.

Jessica   Does that bother you?

Dali   Gala I adore. She is everything. But no, I cannot let her to touch me. Always, I hate to be touched.

Jessica   So have I.

Dali   Is true?

Jessica   Unlike you I find it very painful.

Dali   Touching?

Jessica   Not touching. I pray I shall not have to live my entire life like this.

He stands, she stiffens, he sits again.

She stands and sits beside him. Their hands rise, fall, courting.

Finally they hold hands for about four seconds, then let go.

Dali   How was it for you?

Jessica   Wonderful, thank you.

She moves away, wiping her hand.

Dali   You feel the bones? Is enough sex for Dali. How these ugly millions do this thing to get these gruesome children, all this sucking and prodding and body fluids in and out of one another I will never understand. Inside a beautiful woman is always the putrefying corpse of Dali's passion.

Freud *returns.*

Freud   Are you finished?

Jessica   No. Where's your friend?

Freud   He wished to be left alone. He is a good and powerful man. It is hard to see him powerless.

Jessica   It is hard to believe in good and powerful men, it is so often a contradiction in terms.

Freud   Give me the letters.

Jessica   No.

She leaps up and goes into the closet.

You regret nothing?

Freud   Nothing! Except perhaps one inadvisable evening at *Rookery Nook.*

Jessica   Don't worry, I shan't be in here forever.

Closes and locks the door behind her.

Freud   Then come out for pity's sake! Say what you have to say and leave me alone! Is that what I look like?

Dali To Dali, *si*.

Freud I look dead.

Dali Is no offence. But before you go, please. One thing you do for him.

Freud What?

Dali To judge the work of Dali. The world is a whore, there is no one can tell me. Only you.

Freud Your work?

Dali Please. You see, if this is no good in your eyes ... I have wasted the time of my life. When you look at my paintings, what do you see? Well, you see what I see, obviously, that is the point. But have I caught what we are chasing, you and I? Can you see the unconscious?

Freud Oh, Mr Dali. When I look at a Rembrant, or a classical landscape or a still life by Vermeer, I see a world of unconscious activity. A fountain of hidden dreams.

Dali *Si?*

Freud But when I look at your work I'm afraid all I see is what is conscious. Your ideas, your conceit, your meticulous technique. The conscious rendition of conscious thoughts.

Dali Then this ... He ... I see.

Freud You murder dreams. You understand?

Dali Of course. (*Pause.*) Of course.

Freud I hope I've not offended you.

Dali No, no no. Is just the Death of the Surrealist Movement, is all.

Freud Surely not.

Dali Is no matter, but is caput. You tell me nothing I do not know already. I shall give up the paint.

Freud Oh please, not on account of me.

Dali No, no no ...

Freud   You must continue.

Dali   No. No no no. No. Alright, I shall continue. You and me, we know is shit. But the world is a whore, she will buy the shit. I shall buy a small island.

Freud   Could you spend your life pursuing something you no longer believed in?

Dali   Oh yes, no problem.

Jessica *emerges from the closet.*

Freud *is now genuinely frightened of her.*

Jessica   I'm ready. I have it now. 1897. Who can tell me what is odd about this sentence? 'Those guilty of these infantile seductions are nursemaids, governesses, and domestic servants. Teachers are also involved, as are siblings.' Well?

Dali   Give us a clue.

Jessica   If you like.

She finds another letter.

'The old man died on the night of October 23rd, and we buried him yesterday.' This was your father. 'His death has affected me deeply. By the time he died his life had been long over, but at death the whole past stirs within one.'

Freud   Give them to me.

Jessica   No. Nursemaids, governesses, servants, siblings . . . no mention of fathers, Professor?

Freud   I've had enough of your inquisitory meanderings.

Jessica   I need look no further! I know why you changed your mind. Another letter to Fliess, justifying your decision. Pleading your seduction theory could not stand up because 'In every case of hysteria the father, not even excluding my own, had to be blamed as a pervert.' Not even excluding my own!

Freud   My father was a warm-hearted man possessed of deep wisdom.

Jessica   And?

Freud   I loved and respected him.

Jessica   And.

Freud   This is preposterous.

Jessica   An earlier letter. 'I have now to admit that I have identified signs of psychoneuroses in Marie'. Who was Marie? Marie was your sister.

Freud   The error into which I fell was a bottomless pit which could have swallowed us all.

Jessica   Perhaps it should have done. You suspected your father.

Freud   That is quite enough.

Jessica   Your family leave for the summer, you stay alone. You embark on your own self-analysis.

She flicks pages.

Freud   Those letters are private.

Jessica   Analyse this sentence, Professor Freud. 'Not long ago I dreamt that I was feeling over-affectionate towards Matilde (my eldest daughter, aged nine) but her name was Hella and I saw the word Hella in heavy type before me.' I looked up the name. Hella means Holy. You desired that which was holy to you.

Freud   There was no desire. The dream fulfilled my wish to pin down a father as the originator of neurosis.

Jessica   Then you admit you suspected . . .

Freud   My wish to do so! I suspected nothing.

Jessica   But your father dies condemned. And you discover with horror your own complicity in such desires. It's no wonder you chose to denounce your theories!

Freud   I had no choice!

Jessica   Other than denounce your own father! Other than denounce yourself!

Dali   No! This is a great man. And you, miss-prissy-kiss-my-armpit-tightarsed-girlie say this slanderous things no more!

Jessica   It only remains for me to make my findings known.

Freud   To whom?

Jessica   I believe Dr Yahuda may lend a sympathetic ear.

She exits into the garden.

Freud   Come back here!

Jessica   Dr Yahuda!

Dali   She is cast aspersions on integrity of all great men!

Freud   Stop her. Bring me those letters.

Dali   She is need have her head examined!

Dali *pursues.* **Yahuda** *enters through the DS door.* **Dali** *and* **Jessica** *chase around the garden.*

Yahuda   I've mislaid my gasmask. Did I leave it in here?

Freud   I've not seen it.

Yahuda   Maybe on the porch.

Freud   No. I think I saw it in the hall.

Yahuda   I've looked in the hall.

Freud   I'll look with you.

The sound of breaking glass.

Yahuda   What's that?

Freud   ... a bomb.

Yahuda   A bomb!?

Freud   Unexploded. So far. I suggest we take immediate refuge.

Yahuda   In the shelter?

Freud   No! Under the stairs.

Yahuda   Under the what?

Freud *hustles* **Yahuda** *out the door.* **Jessica** *enters through the window. Scrunching through broken glass off.*

Dali (*off*)   You think it discourage Dali you wield at him the greenhouse? No!

She notices the buff envelope on the desk. An idea comes to her. She removes the Moses and Monotheism *text from the envelope and puts the Fliess letters in its place, resealing the envelope. The other text she puts in the maroon file.*

Dali   You must learn to respect for betters and olders and men who struggle in the mind like a silly girl could not begin to do!

As she finishes he bursts in holding a length of hemp rope.

Is swing, from tree. You want to give me papers and shut up and be good girl, or I am fearless with you, *si*?

She picks up a phallic stone figure and swings it. He cowers.

Donta hita the head! Is full of precious stuff!

Enter **Freud**.

Freud   Move the U-bank and tuck yourself well in.

Yahuda (*off*)   This is absurd.

Freud *closes the door behind him.*

Dali   Dali is got her but she grow violent, so best cure her quickly, *si*?

Jessica   There's nothing wrong with me.

Dali   Put this down or be warned.

Jessica   Go to hell.

Dali   OK. You push Dali to employ his superior intellect!

He picks up a similar but much larger figure.

Freud   That phallus is four thousand years old!

She throws hers at **Dali**.

Freud   No!

Dali *catches it but drops his own weapon on his foot.*

Dali   Argh!

Jessica *runs out of the french windows.*

Jessica   Dr Yahuda!

Dali   Alright, now is personal.

He pursues her, taking an even larger figure. **Freud** *picks up the maroon file, hesitates, crosses to the stove, opens the lid, and drops the file in the fire. The fire roars.* **Yahuda** *enters.*

Yahuda   What do you want?

Freud   Nothing.

Yahuda   Not you; her.

Freud   Who?

Yahuda   I heard shouts.

Freud   For the warden. There is a large unexploded bomb in the greenhouse.

Jessica (*off*)   I need your help, Yah . . . (*Hand clamped over her mouth.*) . . . huda!

Yahuda   There, you see?

Freud   No, no. Our local warden is Mr Yahoohaa.

Jessica (*off*)   Yahuda!

Yahuda   I distinctly heard my name.

Freud   Nonsense. It's all in my head. Your head.

Yahuda   Was that a Freudian slip?

Freud   Certainly not.

He trips over the phallus. Picks it up.

You wait here, where it's safe. I shall deal with the bomb.

He rights the phallus, picks up a soda syphon and exits into the garden. **Yahuda** *spots the buff envelope and picks it up. Unable to restrain himself, he takes it to the stove and hesitates.*

Jessica (*off*)   Dr Yahuda!

This spurs him to action. He lifts the lid. **Jessica** *enters, her head bleeding, and tied round the waist by a rope. On the end of the rope, attempting to restrain her,* **Freud** *and* **Dali**.

Jessica   Oh, thank Go . . . no! Don't do that!!

Yahuda   I was er . . . warming my hands!

Jessica   What's that envelope doing in them?

Yahuda   Good grief; thank God you spotted that.

Freud   How dare you!

He takes the envelope from him.

Have you no regard for a man's life work?

Yahuda   Life's work? Senile piffle.

Jessica   There's something you must know. The theory of infantile sexuality is based upon . . .

Freud *puts a gas mask on her.*

Freud   This woman has turned violently psychotic.

She yells her findings unintelligibly.

Freud   In extreme cases I'm afraid only extreme methods will suffice.

Dali *throws* **Jessica** *down and clambers on top of her.*

Dali   Please to calm down like the good little girl should be seen and not heard.

She tries her best to speak.

Yahuda   She seems to have something to say.

Freud   Everything she says is complete nonsense.

Yahuda   As is everything you write.

Freud   A man's words are his legacy, Yahuda. They should not be censored, or destroyed but should stand in their entirety as a legacy to . . .

Checks the contents.

. . . aagh! No, you're right, let's burn the damn stuff.

Yahuda   Bravo!

Jessica   No!

She grabs it. **Dali** *tries to get it off her.*

Dali   Leave this things alone now; is none of little girls'
business.

Freud   Give it to me!

Jessica   Yahuda . . . read this.

She gives the envelope to **Yahuda**.

Yahuda   I've already read it.

Freud *takes the envelope and manages to secure it in a drawer.*

Freud   It has been a very stimulating afternoon, but I must
ask you all to leave now.

Freud *goes for the door. He pulls the handle, but the door has become
rubber-like. It bends without opening.*

Good God.

Dali   How you do this?

Jessica   I will not be silenced.

Freud   Then I shall call the police.

Jessica   I shall go to the papers. The world will know what I
know!

Freud *picks up the phone. It turns into a lobster.*

Freud   Hello? Would you please connect me with . . .
aaaargh!

Yahuda   What the hell is going on here?

Dali   Don't look at me.

Freud, *frightened now, goes for the door, thinks better of it, heads for the
french windows.*

Freud   Everything's fine. But reluctantly I must bring the evening to a close.

He opens the curtains. A train is hurtling across the garden towards him. Steam, bright lights glaring straight ahead, and a piercing whistle.

Freud   Arrgh!

Yahuda   What the devil?

Freud *closes the curtains.*

Yahuda   What was that?

The clock strikes. **Freud**, *terrified, compares his watch. The clock melts.*

What's happening?

Dali   Is the camembert of time and space, no?

A deep dangerous, thunderous music begins, low at first, building.

Jessica   Doctor Yahuda, you have to listen to me . . .

Freud   No! You and I are flesh and blood. She is just a figment of my imagination.

Yahuda *disappears.*

Freud   Ahhh!

Jessica   Dr Yahuda!

Freud   Gone!

Jessica   Then I shall go too. And find someone willing to listen.

Freud   No. No. I'm getting the hang of this now. You are nothing more than a neurotic manifestation . . .

Jessica   Of what?

Freud   Of a buried subconscious . . .

Jessica   Guilt?

Freud   You don't exist. Now get out of my head! House.

The room continues to melt.

Dali   Back in the closet and there to stay.

Jessica   Let me go!

She kicks **Dali** *in the crotch and dashes out of the downstage door. He dives for and catches the rope.*

Dali   Is no panic. He is got her!

Her momentum pulls him out of the room.

Freud   And stay out.

But **Dali** *reappears almost instantly, pulling the rope.*

Dali   Is OK. She not got anywhere.

Freud   Let her go.

Dali   I bring her back.

Freud   No!

Dali   Is no problem.

Freud   Just . . . let the rope go.

Dali   You and me we sort this women out once and for all, si?

Freud   No, please . . .

Dali   Come back here you hysterical bitch!

Freud   Please, don't . . . !

Dali *gives an almighty tug.* **Jessica** *is no longer tied to the rope. Into the room spills a nude* **Woman**. *Glittering music.*

Freud   No.

Dali   Who is this?

Freud   No, please . . .

The **Woman** *moves towards* **Freud**; *he's both attracted and repelled.*

Dali   Is fantastic! But is who?

Freud   Matilde?

Woman   Papa.

Freud   No. Matilde?

The **Woman** *embraces* **Freud**.

Woman Papa.

Freud Oh, my Matilde . . .

The embrace turns sexual.

No.

Dali Is the most desirable, no?

Freud No! Don't touch me.

He disengages.

I never. . . I never even imagined . . .

Woman Papa!

Freud Leave me alone!

*He runs to the window. She pursues him. A train whistle blows in the
garden, and the curtains billow. **Freud** backs away from the window.
The **Woman** tries to embrace him. He avoids her and runs to hide in the
closet. Opens the door and through it topples a cadaverous, festering, half-
man, half-**Corpse**. Screeching music.*

Ahhh!

Dali Aaaargh!

Corpse Sigmund!

Freud God help me.

*The **Corpse** pursues **Freud**. The **Woman** tries to embrace him.
Dali, in terror, clings on to the filing cabinet.*

Woman Papa.

Corpse Sigmund!

*Sounds of shunting trains compete with music; a drowning cacophony.
Grotesque **Images** appear, reminiscent of **Dali**'s work, but relevant to
Freud's doubts, fears and guilts. **Freud** is horrified as the contents of his
unconscious are spilled across the stage.*

*More **Bodies** appear, reminiscent of concentration camp victims, as are
the antique figures being scattered by the **Woman** and the **Corpse**.
Distant chants from the Third Reich. Four **Old Ladies** appear.*

Ladies Sigmund. Siggy. Sigmund.

They make their way to a gas chamber. Heads hung, they undress . . .

Dali *is hit by a swan.* **Freud** *moves to the door but it is suddenly filled by a huge, crippled, faceless* **Patriarch**. *He enters and towers over* **Freud**. *Music descends to a rumble.*

Freud Papa?

Jessica (*off*) Mama?

Woman Papa?

Jessica Mama?

Corpse Sigmund!

The **Patriarch** *lifts his crutch and swings it, striking the cowering* **Freud** *a massive blow on the jaw.* **Freud** *screams in agony and collapses. The* **Patriarch** *pulls on the rope and* **Jessica** *finally spills into the room.*

Jessica Mama? Mama? Mama?

She is grasped and awkwardly embraced by the figure. Her eyes are screwed shut so as not to see his face.

Patriarch Open your eyes.

She shakes her head.

Open your eyes. Then I shall open them for you.

The razor appears in his hand and he cuts open one of her eyes.

Now, do you see?

Music crashes. Lights crash to a tight downlight on **Freud**. *Stillness. Silence.*

Freud Deeper than cancer. The past. And of all the years, the year I looked into myself is the one that has been killing me. In the months of May and April, one by one, I hunted down my fears, and snared them. Throughout the summer, mounted, pinned and labelled each of them. In October; my anger, for the most part, I embalmed. And in December I dissected love. Love has ever since been grey and lifeless flesh to me. But there has been little pain. The past, for the most part, has passed. I chose to think, not feel.

Dali *leans into his light, smiles.*

Dali   Better now?

Freud   Am I dying?

Dali   *Si.*

Freud   And all this?

Dali   Don't blame me for this; is nothing to do with. I tell you already; surrealism is dead. Besides; is impossible to understand.

Dali *gestures. The* **Patriarch***, the* **Woman***, the* **Corpse** *and the* **Old Ladies** *all disappear. The set begins to return to normal.*

Freud   What about you?

Dali   Dali? Is true. He visit you. This was two months ago. And he look at the death in your face of Freud and he understand how many things were at last to end in Europe with the end of your life. But apart from this he visit and . . . nothing happens much.

Freud   Yahuda?

Dali   Many Jews.

Freud   Her?

Dali   She is nothing. Please.

Dali *sits* **Freud** *in his chair.*

Dali   So . . . Dali visits. Freud remembers . . . sleeps. Goodnight.

Exit **Dali***.*

The air-raid all-clear siren sounds. The set completes its return to normal, as do the lights.

Jessica *stands looking at the sleeping* **Freud***.*

Jessica   Professor?

His eyes open.

Were you sleeping?

Freud   I don't believe so.

Jessica   I'm sorry I got angry.

Freud   To get angry is most necessary.

Jessica   But people get hurt.

Freud   If the anger is . . .

Jessica   Children get hurt.

Freud   . . . appropriately expressed, no one gets hurt.

Pause.

Jessica   Do you still insist my mother was never molested by my grandfather?

Freud   No, she was not.

Jessica   Well, that's a remarkable thing.

Freud   Why?

Jessica   Because I was. And please don't suggest that I imagined this. He was no beloved, half-desired father to me. He was a wiry old man who smelt of beer and cheese and would limp to my bed and masturbate on me. Only once was it an unexpected thing. And once he whispered if I told my father, he would do worse to me with this.

She shows the razor.

My mother knew what he would do, if she were not there to listen for the door, the creaking stair. That's why she protested at being sent away. And so fierce and vehement her protest, sent away she surely was.

Freud *bows his head.*

Jessica   What was it you remembered in your self-analysis, Professor? About your father?

Freud   What is more relevant is what I could not remember.

Jessica   Have you no feelings?

Freud I chose to think. And if now I am not so much a man as a museum, and my compassion just another dulled exhibit, so be it. All I have done, what I've become . . . was necessary. To set the people free.

Jessica Dead already.

Freud Oh, a few bats hang in the tower; fear. The odd rat still scampers through the basement; guilt. Other than that the building is silent.

Jessica Liar.

Freud I hear nothing.

Jessica You heard me.

Freud Nothing.

Jessica Listen harder.

Freud *breaks down. Weeps.*

Jessica What? What is it?

Freud The exhibits are screaming.

Jessica Goodbye.

Freud I don't know your name.

Jessica Jessica.

Freud God is looking.

Jessica Goodbye.

Freud Jessica. The young may speak what the old cannot bear to utter.

Jessica Because I can articulate these things does not mean I am able to bear them.

She leaves. **Yahuda** *enters and examines the chessboard.* **Freud** *speaks with difficulty.*

Freud Yahuda?

Yahuda Freud?

Freud   You will remember you promised to help me when the time came. Well, it's torture now.

Yahuda *nods.*

Yahuda   Have you spoken to Anna?

Freud   She will understand.

Yahuda *nods. From his bag he takes a hypodermic, prepares it, and injects* **Freud** *with two centigrammes of morphine.*

Freud   Thank you, my friend. In the drawer. There are some letters to Fliess.

Yahuda   I have them.

Freud   The one on top.

Yahuda   Yes?

Freud   Take a pen. A pen; use ink. From the word 'father'.

Yahuda   Yes?

Freud   Delete for me five words. 'Not even excluding my own.'

Yahuda   Done.

Freud   Illegible?

Yahuda   Gone.

Freud   Thank you.

He closes his eyes. Grimaces.

Yahuda   I shall repeat the dose in twelve hours, if necessary. Whatever is required. You may hallucinate. Don't be afraid.

The grimace tightens, then the drug takes hold.

Freud   Oh ... heaven.

And **Freud**'s *face relaxes as he falls into a sleep which will become his last.*

Yahuda *dismisses a tear, takes a last move at the chessboard and leaves quietly.*

The sound of rain beyond the window, and a subtle change of light.

Freud *wakes. Looks at his watch.*

Freud   If you are waiting for me to break the silence you will be deeply disappointed. The silence is yours alone, and is far more eloquent than you might imagine.

He turns in his chair and looks towards the couch. Frowns when he sees there is no one on it.

Jessica *appears through the rain and stops outside the french windows. Her hair hangs dripping to her shoulders.*

She taps on the glass. **Freud** *looks at her. Closes his eyes, too tired to go through all this again, but knowing he may have to.*

Jessica *continues to tap as the lights fade.*

A SELECTED LIST OF
METHUEN MODERN PLAYS

Methuen Contemporary Dramatists
include

Peter Barnes (three volumes)
Sebastian Barry
Edward Bond (six volumes)
Howard Brenton
  (two volumes)
Richard Cameron
Jim Cartwright
Caryl Churchill (two volumes)
Sarah Daniels (two volumes)
David Edgar (three volumes)
Dario Fo (two volumes)
Michael Frayn (two volumes)
Peter Handke
Jonathan Harvey
Declan Hughes
Terry Johnson
Bernard-Marie Koltès
Doug Lucie
David Mamet (three volumes)

Anthony Minghella
  (two volumes)
Tom Murphy (four volumes)
Phyllis Nagy
Peter Nichols (two volumes)
Philip Osment
Louise Page
Stephen Poliakoff
  (three volumes)
Christina Reid
Philip Ridley
Willy Russell
Ntozake Shange
Sam Shepard (two volumes)
David Storey (three volumes)
Sue Townsend
Michel Vinaver (two volumes)
Michael Wilcox

Methuen World Classics
include

Jean Anouilh (two volumes)
John Arden (two volumes)
Arden & D'Arcy
Brendan Behan
Aphra Behn
Bertolt Brecht (six volumes)
Büchner
Bulgakov
Calderón
Anton Chekhov
Noël Coward (five volumes)
Eduardo De Filippo
Max Frisch
Gorky
Harley Granville Barker
    (two volumes)
Henrik Ibsen (six volumes)
Lorca (three volumes)
Marivaux

Mustapha Matura
David Mercer (two volumes)
Arthur Miller (five volumes)
Molière
Musset
Clifford Odets
Joe Orton
A. W. Pinero
Luigi Pirandello
Terence Rattigan
W. Somerset Maugham
    (two volumes)
Wole Soyinka
August Strindberg
    (three volumes)
J. M. Synge
Ramón del Valle-Inclán
Frank Wedekind
Oscar Wilde